Look-Alikes

CONTENTS

NATIONAL GEOGRAPHIC   Hampton-Brown

School Publishing

Words with u_e

Look at each picture. Read the words.

u_e

Example:

c**u**b**e**

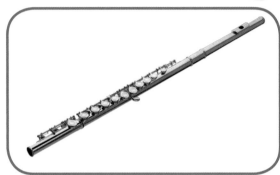

fl**u**te

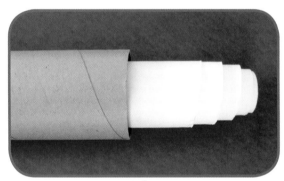

t**u**b**e**

h**u**g**e** pack

m**u**le

d**u**n**e**

High Frequency Words

four
may
only
other
show
some

Key Words

Look at the pictures. Read the riddle.
Talk with a partner to find the answer.

What Is It?

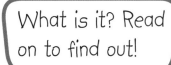
What is it? Read on to find out!

1. It has **four** legs.

2. **Some** **may** be just black.

3. **Others** **may** be **only** tan.

4. The huge ears **show** what it is!

Phonics Games
NGReach.com

3

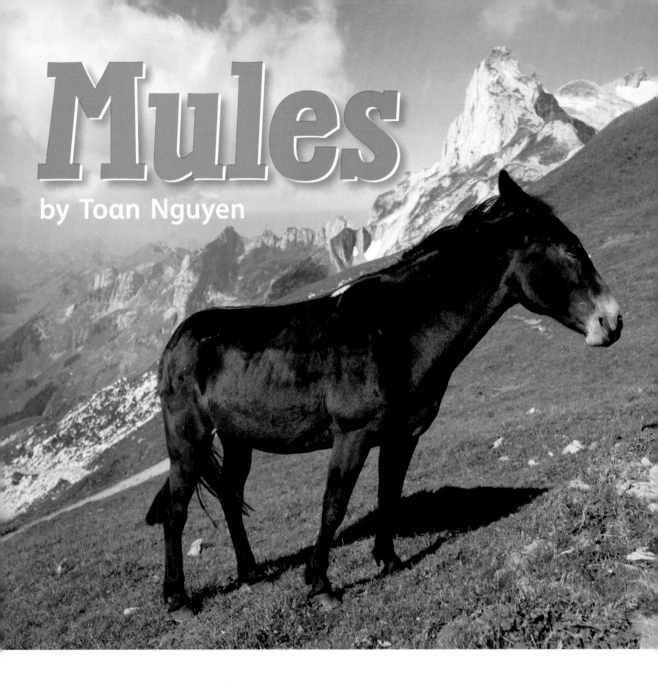

Mules

by Toan Nguyen

What animal is this?

It can be huge. It has four legs.
It has big ears.

Is it a horse? Are you sure?

It looks a bit like a horse, but not

just like a horse. Its mother is a horse.

Is it a donkey? Are you sure?

It looks a bit like a donkey, but not

just like a donkey. Its dad is a donkey.

It is the only animal like it. Do you think it is cute?

It's a bit like a horse. It's a bit like a donkey.

It's a mule!

A mule can carry a big pack. You may take a mule on a ride. You can show it where to go. Jump on! ❖

Words with u_e

Read these words.

cute	mole	mule	huge
gum	cube	jump	pack

Find the words with **u_e**.
Use letters to build them.

m u l e

Choose words from the
box above to tell a partner
about each picture.

A _mule_ can
be _cute_ .

e   e_e

Words with Long e

Look at each picture. Read the words.

This is me.

We play a game.

Pete is my pal.

She is my mom.

High Frequency
Words

| four |
| may |
| only |
| other |
| show |
| some |

Key Words

Read the sentences. Match each sentence to one of the pictures.

Ladybugs

1. **Some** ladybugs **may** have **only four** dots.
2. **Other** ladybugs have more than four dots.
3. A ladybug **shows** its six legs.

All ladybugs have six legs.

GO! **Phonics Games**
NGReach.com

Ladybugs

by Anne Kate Mead
illustrated by Julia Woolf

Steve and Pete are twins. Pete wants
to go on a bug hunt.

 We'll look for some bugs, Steve!

Steve saw a bug. It was red with black spots.

 Look at this cute ladybug!

 Let me see, Steve.

Dad's home, Pete. Let's ask him if he can show us his bug book.

 Look at this page. A ladybug has eggs in the spring. Next, the eggs hatch.

 Only this looks like a ladybug.

 She looks like some other bug.

But she does not look like a ladybug.

Not yet. She may rest for a while. Then she will look like a ladybug.

 Here they are.

 Two ladybugs, Pete!

 Twins! ❖

Words with Long <u>e</u>

Read these words.

Steve	it	she	red
me	Jen	he	hen

Find words with long **e**.
Use letters to build them.

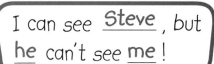

Talk Together

Choose words from the box above to talk about what you see.

I can see <u>Steve</u> , but <u>he</u> can't see <u>me</u> !

In the Garden

Look at the picture with a partner. Take turns reading the clues. Find the answers in the picture.

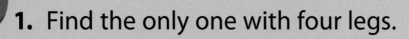

1. Find the only one with four legs.
2. Find some bugs that may sting.
3. Find a huge flower.
4. Find the rake.
5. Find a cute stone pot.
6. Find a place we can sit with Pete the cat.
7. Find the other place we can sit.

Acknowledgments

Grateful acknowledgment is given to the authors, artists, photographers, museums, publishers, and agents for permission to reprint copyrighted material. Every effort has been made to secure the appropriate permission. If any omissions have been made or if corrections are required, please contact the Publisher.

Photographic Credits

CVR (Cover) Juniors Bildarchiv/Alamy Images.**2** (bl) Robert Bremec/iStockphoto. (br) Jacques Jangaoux/Mira.com. (tl) Carlos Restrepo/iStockphoto. (tr) Artville. **3** (b) Liz Garza Williams/ Hampton-Brown/National Geographic School Publishing. (cl) Juan Manuel Borrero/Nature Picture Library. (cr) blickwinkel/Alamy Images. (tl) Biosphoto / Klein J.-L. & Hubert M.-L./ Peter Arnold, Inc.. (tr) Biosphoto/Jimenez Saez Jose Antonio/Peter Arnold, Inc.. **4** Robert Maier/Animals Animals. **5** allen russell/Alamy Images. **6** Kseniya Abramova/iStockphoto. **7** WILDLIFE/Peter Arnold, Inc.. **8** Richard Goerg/iStockphoto. **9** Chris Rogers/Index Stock/ age fotostock. **10** (b) Christine Pemberton/The Image Works, Inc.. (tl) Holger Leue/Lonely Planet Images. (tr) ARCO / Loos K/Arco Images/age fotostock. **11** (bc) ARCO/H Reinhard/ Arco Images/age fotostock. (bl) Grant Heilman/Grant Heilman Photography. (br) Black Star/ Alamy Images. (t) Liz Garza Williams/Hampton-Brown/National Geographic School Publishing. **13** (b) Liz Garza Williams/Hampton-Brown/National Geographic School Publishing. (tc) Jim Schemel/iStockphoto. (tl) Stanko Mravljak/iStockphoto. (tr) Robert P. Carr/Bruce Coleman Inc./ Photoshot. **21** (bc) Rob Marmion/Shutterstock. (bl) PhotoDisc/Getty Images. (br) Iain Sarjeant/ iStockphoto. (t) Liz Garza Williams/Hampton-Brown/National Geographic School Publishing.

Illustrator Credits
12, 22-23 Jannie Ho; **14-20** Julia Woolf

The National Geographic Society
John M. Fahey, Jr., President & Chief Executive Officer
Gilbert M. Grosvenor, Chairman of the Board

National Geographic School Publishing
Hampton-Brown
www.NGSP.com

Printed in the USA.
RR Donnelley, Jefferson City, MO

ISBN:978-0-7362-8037-2

13 14 15 16 17 18 19
10 9 8 7 6 5